Creative Napkins

& Table Settings

Jimmy Ng
with Melissa Rhone

Photography by
Jimmy Ng

Schiffer
Publishing Ltd

4880 Lower Valley Road • Atglen, PA 19310

Other Schiffer Books on Related Subjects:
Entertaining with Flowers: The Floral Artistry of Bill Murphy. Bill Murphy, AIFD.
ISBN: 978-0-7643-2556-4. $29.95

Copyright © 2013 by Jimmy Ng

Library of Congress Control Number: 2013935531

Designed by RoS
Type set in Boulevard/Parisine Plus Std Clair

ISBN: 978-0-7643-4401-5
Printed in China

Published by Schiffer Publishing, Ltd.
4880 Lower Valley Road
Atglen, PA 19310
Phone: (610) 593-1777; Fax: (610) 593-2002
E-mail: Info@schifferbooks.com

For the largest selection of fine reference books on this and related subjects,
please visit our website at **www.schifferbooks.com.** You may also write for a free
catalog.

This book may be purchased from the publisher.
Please try your bookstore first.

We are always looking for people to write books on new and related subjects. If
you have an idea for a book, please contact us at
proposals@schifferbooks.com

Schiffer Books are available at special discounts for bulk purchases for sales
promotions or premiums. Special editions, including personalized covers,
corporate imprints, and excerpts can be created in large quantities for special
needs. For more information contact the publisher.

In Europe, Schiffer books are distributed by
Bushwood Books
6 Marksbury Ave.
Kew Gardens
Surrey TW9 4JF England
Phone: 44 (0) 20 8392 8585; Fax: 44 (0) 20 8392 9876
E-mail: info@bushwoodbooks.co.uk
Website: www.bushwoodbooks.co.uk

Seamless Wallpaper, Vector Background © Ozerina Anna
(www.bigstock.com)

> "*Guests* experience the table design
> before the meal.
> Once seated, their impression
> of the tabletop sets expectations
> for the meal to come."
>
> —*Jimmy Ng*

Contents

Introduction

Inviting someone into your home for a meal or party can say a lot about you, which is why selecting the dishes, flatware and glassware, napkins, tablecloths, and table decorations is an important task for any host or hostess. The goal of this book is to help make those tasks easier.

Many people fail to realize that beautifully folded napkins are functional works of art that add life to any table. They make party guests feel special and serve as conversation starters, yet can still be used to wipe up spills and prevent stains.

It's easy to be intimidated by napkin art. Don't be! While some napkin folds are a bit intricate and more advanced, there are plenty of basic folds that are simple to learn. Once you master those, you can move on to fancier folds. Any type of napkin fold can serve as the basis for a creative table setting.

One thing is critical regardless of your level of napkin-folding expertise—handle napkins in the same manner you would prepare food. Always wash your hands before handling napkins and be sure to prepare them on a clean surface.

Types of Napkins

Napkins are available in a variety of materials. Paper napkins are convenient and inexpensive, while cloth napkins offer an air of sophistication and easily add a touch of class to any meal.

There are multiple types of cloth napkins. Linen napkins are great to use for formal dinners because they provide a superior look. Cotton napkins are softer than linen napkins and perfect for everyday home use. Polyester napkins work well for busy families and casual meals. They are also iron-free.

Taking Care of Your Napkins

Cloth napkins are reusable, but it's important to take proper care of them. Wash your napkins with mild detergent only. After washing the napkins, I recommend removing them from the dryer when they are still damp and hanging them up to air dry. Napkins can shrink in the dryer! It's also best to iron your napkins when they are still a bit damp because this allows you to stretch them back to their full size.

Many people struggle with the question of how much starch to use on their cloth napkins. I prefer medium starch, because using more starch means the napkins will be harder on your guests' mouths. If you are new to the art of napkin folding and prefer to use more starch, try ironing to create the crease instead.

Napkin Sizes

Have you ever noticed that cloth napkins come in different sizes? I prefer the following sizes for the following meals:

- Dinner: 22-inch napkins
- Lunch: 20-inch napkins
- Breakfast: 18- or 20-inch napkins

If you aren't certain what size napkins you have and there's not a ruler handy, a rule of thumb is to remember that napkins will be placed on your lap. A napkin that is too small to cover your lap can possibly lead to spills and stains, and no party host wants guests to drop food onto their clothing during a meal at their home! Some antique cloth hand towels and modern extra-large napkins can cover the entire lap. They are often referred to as "lapkins."

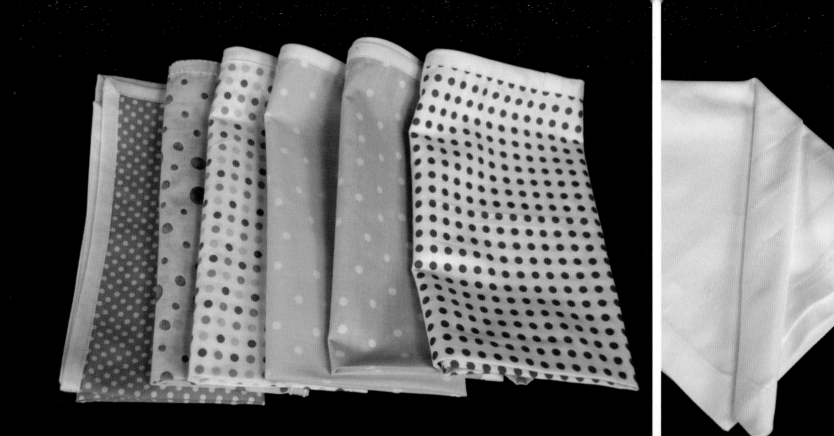

Napkin Folding Tips

The best size napkin for fancy folds is 22-inch. Linen and cotton both work well for stand-up napkin folds, but napkin rings can also help napkins stay upright. You must also take your party or event's location into consideration, as outdoor table settings could be affected by weather conditions, such as wind. Again, napkin rings or even ribbons are good ways to help your napkins stay intact. Flowers or place cards can decorate the napkins, yet double as weights that help hold them down. Last-minute party preparations can be stressful, but it is possible to prepare your napkins ahead of time. Evenly-sprayed starch can help them stay in place.

Place Setting Diagram: When setting the table for a formal meal, it's easy to get confused about what goes where. This place setting diagram will come in handy if you want to follow the traditional rules for a formal place setting, but there's no need to worry about every single detail. If you don't own a particular type of flatware or glassware, make substitutions. Be creative!

PEPPER   SALT

WATER

BUTTER KNIFE

DESSERT FORK & SPOON

RED WINE

BREAD & BUTTER PLATE

WHITE WINE

SHERRY

NAPKIN

DINNER PLATE

FISH FORK   DINNER FORK   SALAD FORK

DINNER KNIFE   FISH KNIFE   SOUP SPOON   OYSTER FORK

CHARGER PLATE

A Bow

A great addition to traditional holiday dinners or birthday parties, A Bow napkin fold can help turn any meal into a true gift between friends and family.

1. Fold the napkin into a triangle by lifting the bottom corner to meet the top corner.

2. Fold the top corner down until it meets the napkin's bottom edge, creating a small triangle.

3. Fold the top section about 1/3 of the way down.

4. Lift the bottom section about 1/3 of the way up.

5. Roll the napkin in half so it will fit into a napkin ring.

6. Slide one end of the napkin into a napkin ring and pull it through.

7. Repeat with the other end of the napkin and adjust as necessary until it resembles a bow.

8. Reverse the folded napkin so that the bow is right side up.

Martha

American Eagle

Suitable for military wedding receptions, Fourth of July festivities, or any event highlighting Americana, the American Eagle napkin fold instantly adds a patriotic touch to the table.

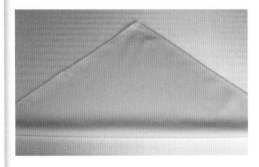

1. Fold the napkin into a triangle by lifting the bottom corner to meet the top corner.

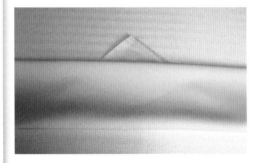

2. Lift the napkin from the bottom up until a small triangle is sticking out at the top.

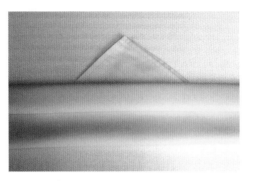

3. Leaving the small triangle intact, roll 1/3 of the folded napkin downward to create a small cuff.

4. Create three small accordion-like ruffles on the right side of the napkin by gathering the cloth with your fingers. Be sure to leave excess cloth on the end as this will be the eagle's wing.

5. Repeat step number four with the left side of the napkin and create two additional ruffles. This gathered cloth meets in the middle to form the eagle's body.

6. Carefully tuck the folded napkin into a cup or glass with the eagle's wings protruding over the edges. If desired, decorate the eagle with adhesive wiggle eyes and a triangular-shaped piece of felt to imply a beak.

Baby Onesie

The Baby Onesie napkin fold will have your baby shower guests cooing over its cuteness.

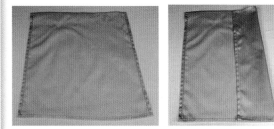

1. Place the napkin face down in front of you.

2. Fold the right side of the napkin inward until it reaches the center

3. Fold the left side of the napkin inward, slightly overlapping the center of the napkin.

4. Fold the top left corner of the napkin downward into a triangle, letting it slightly hang over the napkin's edge.

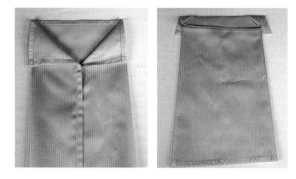

5. Repeat the process on the right side. Fold the right top corner of the napkin downward, letting it slightly hang over the napkin's edge. This will resemble a shirt collar.

6. Turn the napkin over and fold the top flap of the napkin approximately 1/2-inch downward.

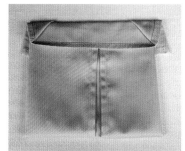

7. Lift the bottom of the napkin upward and tuck it under the flap.

8. Turn the napkin over once again so that the "collar" is facing you.

9. Gently lift the bottom right side of the napkin and tuck the bottom right corner inward.

10. Close the "flap" and flatten the bottom right side with your hand.

11. Repeat the process on the bottom left side of the napkin. If desired, decorate the baby onesie with a bow and buttons.

A classic napkin fold that is often seen at wedding receptions and other graceful galas, the Bird of Paradise adds elegance and sophistication to any dining experience.

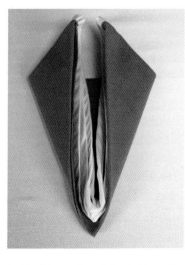

1. Fold the napkin into quarters and place it with the open sides pointing upward.

3. Fold the left and right sides of the napkin inward so they meet in the middle, creating a kite-like shape.

5. Turn the napkin counter-clockwise so the pointed end is on the left.

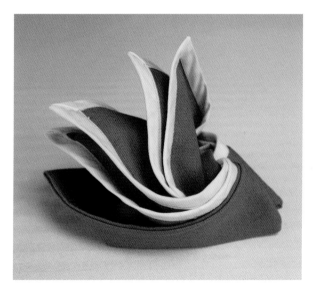

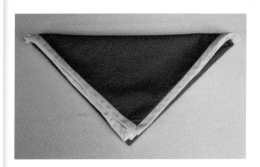

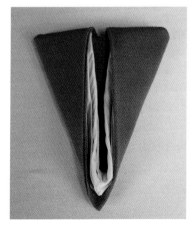

2. Fold the top corner down until it meets the bottom corner, creating a triangle.

4. Tuck the top ends of the napkin underneath to create a flat line along the top.

6. Hold the right side of the napkin and use your left hand to gently pull the layers that your fold created upward, one at a time. Adjust the layers as necessary.

Bunny in a Hat

Perfect for Easter brunch or any other springtime celebration, Bunny in a Hat will delight both the young and the young at heart.

1. Fold the napkin in half so that the open end is at the bottom.

2. Fold the bottom left corner upward, resulting in a triangle.

3. Fold the top right corner downward, resulting in a triangle.

4. Turn the napkin over and place it so it resembles a trapezoid.

5. Lift the bottom right edge of the napkin upward until it meets the top edge. Carefully pull the excess fabric downward, resulting in a triangle on the right side.

6. Tuck the top left corner underneath the triangle on the right side, resulting in a smaller triangle on the left side.

7. Turn the napkin over.

8. Carefully tuck the right corner into the pocket on the left side.

9. Fold the top right corner down by reversing the napkin.

10. Fold the top left corner down by reversing the napkin.

11. Carefully stand the napkin upright and gently separate the sides to create a bowl shape. Insert Bunny!

Resembling an opened envelope, the Diamond Fold flawlessly complements the most elegant affairs, yet instantly adds a touch of class to casual get-togethers.

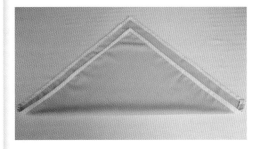

1. Fold the napkin into a triangle by lifting the bottom corner toward the top corner, leaving approximately 1/2-inch between the corners as seen.

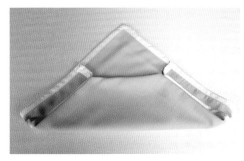

3. Fold the bottom of the napkin halfway up.

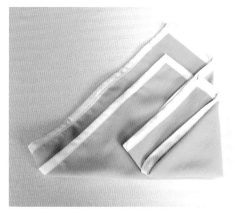

5. Fold the right side of the napkin inward.

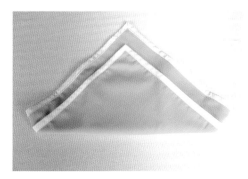

4. Turn the folded napkin over.

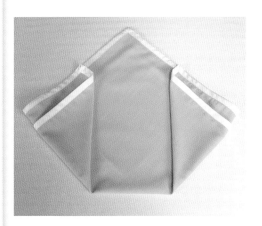

2. Turn the napkin over and fold the left side upward to create a small triangle. Repeat on the right side.

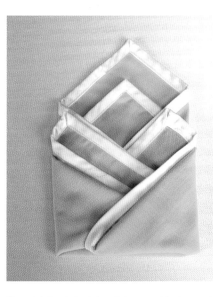

6. Fold the left side of the napkin inward and tuck it inside the small pocket that was created when the right side was folded inward.

Named with Elton John's touching tribute to Princess Diana in mind, the England's Rose napkin fold can make a graceful addition to romantic dinners or special family gatherings.

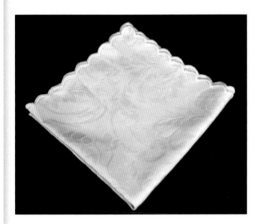

1. Fold the napkin into quarters and place it with the open sides pointing upward.

2. Fold the top corner down until it meets the bottom corner, creating a triangle.

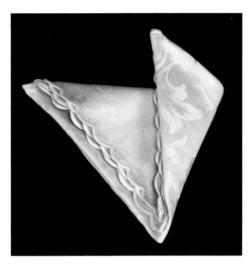

3. Fold the right side of the napkin inward.

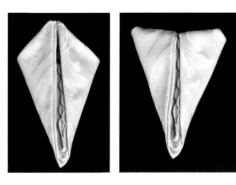

4. Repeat with the left side of the napkin, resulting in a kite-like shape.

5. Tuck the top tip of the napkin underneath to create a flat line, resulting in a triangle.

6. Turn the napkin so that it is pointing toward the left.

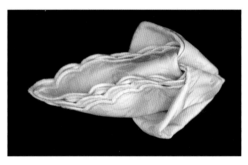

7. Hold the right side of the napkin with your right hand. Use your left hand to reverse the bottom layer and fold it under.

8. Gently pull out the layers that your fold created upward, one at a time. Adjust the layers as necessary. Tuck the bloom of a rose inside to complete the England's Rose fold.

Four-Leaf Clover

Add a bit of magical charm to the table with the Four-Leaf Clover napkin fold, a perfect choice whenever you need a little "luck of the Irish" on your side.

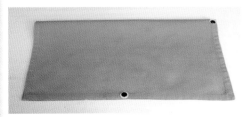

1. Fold the napkin in half so that the open end is at the bottom.

2. Take the top right corner and tuck it inside the napkin.

3. Repeat the process on the left side. Take the top left corner of the napkin and tuck it inside the napkin, resulting in a triangle.

4. Turn the napkin so that the triangle is pointing downward. Fold the top right flap inward.

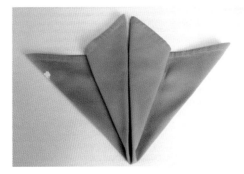

5. Repeat the process on the left side. Fold the top left flap inward.

6. Fold the bottom flaps inward as well, resulting in a kite-like shape.

7. Tuck the top of the "kite" downward behind the napkin.

8. Turn the napkin over. Fold it in half by grabbing the middle cone shape and opening the top flaps to create the four-leaf clover. Adjust as necessary.

Irene

Jared the Doll

Jared the Doll is a popular napkin fold for birthday parties and other children's events. It's fun, yet adds a touch of charm that parents will appreciate.

1. Place the napkin face down in front of you.

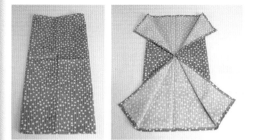

2. Fold both sides of the napkin inward until they meet in the middle.

3. Lift all four corners of the napkin and pull them outward, creating triangle-shaped flaps.

4. Roll the bottom of the napkin upward. Stop when you reach the center.

5. Repeat the process and roll the top of the napkin downward. Stop when you reach the bottom roll.

6. Grasp the left end of the rolled napkin and tuck 1/3 inside. Turn the napkin over and lay it vertically.

7. Fold the napkin in half with both hands on the sides, adjusting as necessary.

8. Tuck flatware inside the napkin so that the spoon implies Jared the Doll's head.

Kiss

Faintly resembling a pair of lips, the Kiss napkin fold is stunning both on its own or embellished with a flower.

1. Fold the napkin into quarters and place it with the open sides pointing upward.

2. Fold the top corner down until it meets the bottom corner, creating a triangle.

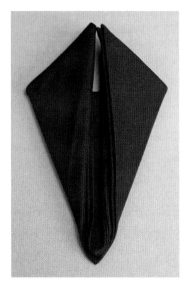

3. Fold the left and right sides of the napkin inward so they meet in the middle, creating a kite-like shape.

4. Tuck the top ends of the napkin underneath to create a flat line along the top.

5. Turn the napkin around.

6. Turn the napkin over as shown in the photo. Fold it in half and continue holding with one hand. The flaps are now in the center.

7. While still holding the napkin with your right hand, pull the top down gently. Adjust as necessary.

Britney

McEntire's Double Fantasy

The McEntire's Double Fantasy is a unique fan-like napkin fold that is perfect for formal holiday meals.

1. Place the napkin face down in front of you.

2. Start at the bottom and fold the napkin as you would fold a paper fan, making alternating rows that are approximately one-inch thick. Do this until you have two inches of fabric remaining at the top of the napkin. It might be helpful to use a weighted object to keep the bottom row of folds in place.

3. Turn the napkin over and fold the right side downward.

4. Repeat the process and fold down the left side of the napkin.

5. Turn the napkin over so that the point is facing you and the accordion-like rows are underneath.

6. Fold the right side of the napkin downward.

7. Repeat the process and fold the left side of the napkin downward.

8. Carefully open the napkin, pulling the accordion-like rows upward. The finished product should resemble two open paper fans sitting side by side.

Montana

The Montana napkin fold is simple to learn yet helps turn any table setting from *drab* to *designer*.

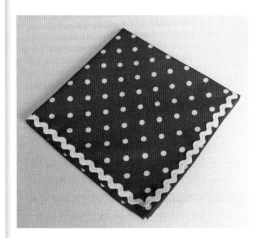

1. Fold the napkin into quarters and place it with the open sides pointing downward.

2. Pull the left and right sides into the center of the napkin.

3. Tuck about 1/3 of the top of the napkin underneath to create a flat line along the top.

4. Carefully hold the napkin and push both sides up from underneath.

My Butterfly

Dainty and whimsical, My Butterfly helps transform even the most basic meals into cheerful summertime celebrations.

1. Fold the napkin into a triangle by bringing the bottom corner down to meet the top corner.

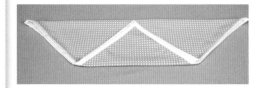

2. Fold the bottom corner up until it meets the napkin's top edge, creating a small triangle.

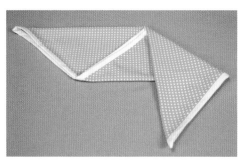

3. Fold the right side of the napkin downward.

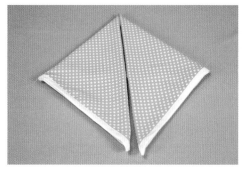

4. Repeat the process and fold the left side of the napkin downward.

5. Fold the napkin into a triangle by tucking the bottom of the napkin underneath, making a straight edge along the bottom.

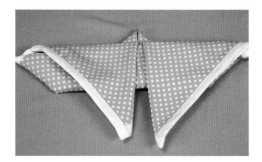

6. Roll the bottom of the napkin upward and leave a small triangle shape exposed.

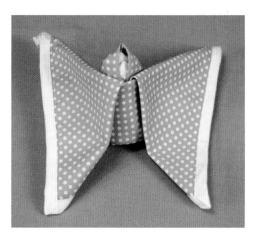

7. Fold the napkin in half and smooth down the flaps on both sides to create the butterfly's wings. Apply pipe cleaner antennae if desired.

My Zebra

My Zebra is proof that any fold can receive an instant makeover with the use of a patterned napkin.

1. Fold the napkin in half so that the open end is at the bottom.

2. Fold the top left and right corners downward until they meet in the middle, resulting in a large triangle comprised of two smaller triangles.

3. Fold the bottom right corner downward.

4. Repeat the process on the left side. Fold the bottom left corner downward as well, resulting in a kite-like shape.

5. Fold the top of the "kite" downward behind the napkin to create a flat line along the top.

6. Fold the napkin in half and gently fan the left and right flaps outward, adjusting as necessary. Tuck the bloom of a flower into the center for added beauty.

Flowers can easily improve the appearance of any dinner table. The *Orchid in Bloom* napkin fold does just that.

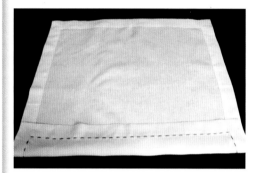

1. Place the napkin face down in front of you. Start at the bottom and fold the napkin 6 times, making alternating rows that are approximately 3 inches thick.

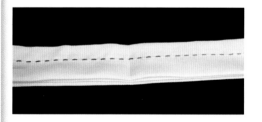

2. Smooth the folded napkin down in front of you. You should have 3 layers.

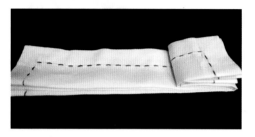

3. Fold the napkin in half to create a center crease as your guide. Pull the right side of the napkin to the center crease and lay the other half down.

4. Repeat the process on the opposite side. You now have 2 small squares.

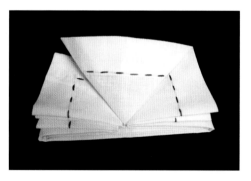

5. Pull the top flap on the right side upward toward the center.

6. Tuck the napkin flap inside itself.

7. Repeat the process with the second and third flap on the right side.

8. Do this with the left side as well. Gently separate the folded flaps to create a fan-like bloom in the center of the napkin. Place a fresh orchid in the center of the bloom.

Party Dress

What a doll! Simple to learn, the Party Dress napkin fold can add some pizzazz to any party!

3. Place a small rubber band around the top of the folded napkin. Fan out the top and bottom sections so that they resemble a party dress.

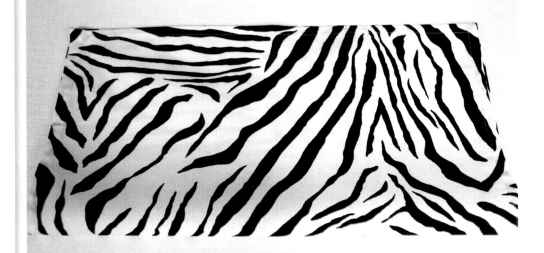

1. Fold the napkin in half so that the open end is at the top.

2. Turn the napkin sideways. Start at the bottom and fold the napkin as you would fold a paper fan, making alternating rows that are approximately 1-inch thick.

4. Hide the rubber band with a small flower or some other embellishment. Place the finished napkin on top of a Barbie® or similar doll if desired.

Rabbit

Hop into spring with a little help from the adorable Rabbit napkin fold. It's perfect for the kids' table on Easter Sunday.

1. Fold the napkin into a triangle by lifting the bottom corner toward the top corner.

2. Fold the top corner down until it meets the napkin's bottom edge, creating a small triangle.

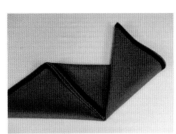

3. Fold the right side of the napkin upward.

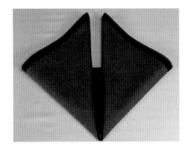

4. Repeat the process and fold the left side of the napkin upward. Leave a small gap down the center.

5. Fold the far right corner of the napkin inward toward the center, creating a small triangle. Use a paper clip to hold the triangle in place.

6. Repeat the process and fold the far left corner of the napkin inward toward the center, creating another small triangle. Use a paper clip to hold the triangle in place.

7. Turn the napkin over.

8. Gently tug the top right corner of the napkin downward to create an ear.

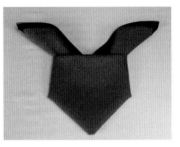

9. Gently tug the top left corner of the napkin downward to create the rabbit's other ear.

10. Fold the bottom point of the napkin underneath to create a flat edge. If desired, decorate the rabbit with adhesive wiggle eyes and craft supplies to create its face.

Show that special someone just how much you care with the Real Love napkin fold. Embellish with flowers for extra beauty or use as-is.

1. Fold the napkin into a triangle by lifting the bottom corner to meet the top corner.

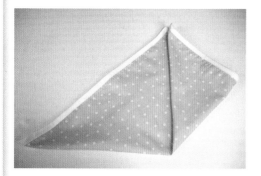

2. Fold the right side of the napkin inward.

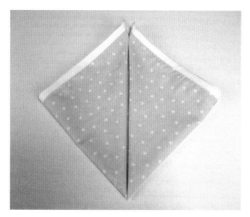

3. Repeat with the left side of the napkin.

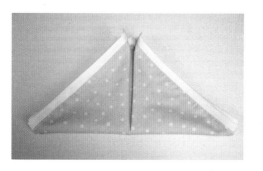

4. Tuck the bottom half of the napkin into the back of the napkin to create a triangle.

5. Fold both of the top corners of the triangle downward, resulting in flaps that resemble petals.

6. Holding both flaps as you tuck them to the sides of the center flaps, gently push the center flaps up.

Seal of Love

Romantic dinners aren't just for Valentine's Day, and the Seal of Love napkin fold is a great alternative to traditional hearts and flowers.

1. Fold the napkin into quarters and place it with the open sides pointing upward.

2. Fold the top corner of the napkin downward, resulting in a triangle.

3. Fold the next layer downward, creating a second triangle. Be sure there is a small gap between the triangles.

4. Fold the third layer downward. Be sure to leave a small gap this time as well.

5. Turn the napkin over.

6. Fold the right side of the napkin inward, creating a triangle.

7. Repeat the process and fold the left side of the napkin inward.

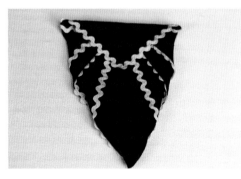

8. Fold the top point of the napkin down until it meets the top edge of both triangles. "Seal" the napkin with a small flower or other decorative object heavy enough to keep the flap weighted down.

Hosting a Bon Voyage party? Let *all* of your guests take a "dinner cruise" with the adorable Ship napkin fold.

1. Fold the napkin into quarters and place it with the open sides pointing upward. Fold the top corner downward, tucking the napkin inside itself and creating a small pocket.

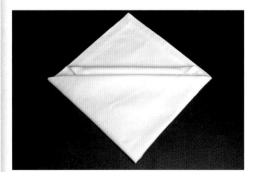

2. Fold the next layer of the napkin downward, once again tucking the napkin inside itself. Leave a small gap to create the levels of the cruise ship.

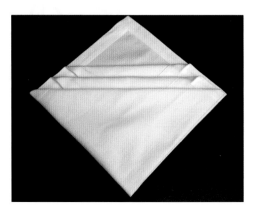

3. Repeat this process. Fold the third layer of the napkin downward, once again tucking the napkin inside itself. You should now have 3 visible "ship levels."

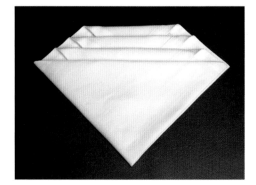

4. Fold the final layer of the napkin downward, creating a flat edge along the top of the napkin. You should now have 4 visible "ship levels."

5. Fold the napkin to the back, showing a triangle on the top.

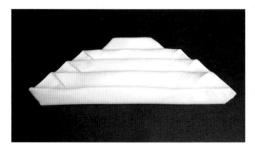

6. Fold the top point of the napkin downward to create a flat edge along the top. Decorate the ship with ribbon and stickers to create portholes and a smokestack.

Spaceship

Blast into outer space with the Spaceship, a great way to let friends and family know you're over the moon for them!

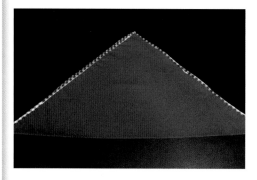

1. Fold the napkin into a triangle by lifting the bottom corner to meet the top corner.

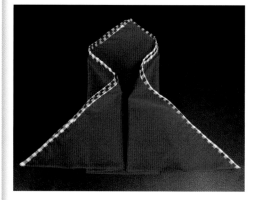

2. Fold the left and right sides into the center of the napkin, creating a flap on each side.

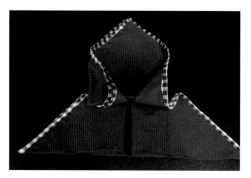

3. Gently pull the top section of the napkin downward, creating a small cuff that rests on top of the flaps.

4. Tuck the right flap behind the napkin.

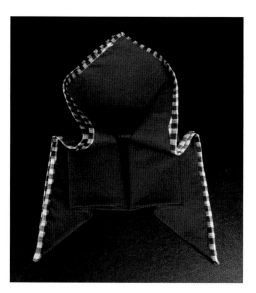

5. Repeat the process and tuck the left flap behind the napkin. Decorate with place cards or USA labels if desired.

Quickly turn any party into a beach party with the Starfish napkin fold.

1. Place the napkin face down in front of you.

2. Fold the napkin into a triangle by lifting the bottom corner to meet the top corner.

3. Fold the right side of the napkin inward.

4. Repeat with the left side of the napkin.

5. Fold the napkin in half.

6. Carefully stand the napkin on the table and slightly twist each flap to create the starfish shape. Adjust as necessary.

The Sushi napkin fold looks good enough to eat. It's a true conversation starter, especially when Japanese food is on the menu.

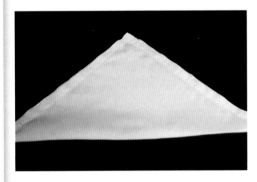

1. Fold the napkin into a triangle by lifting the bottom corner to meet the top corner.

2. Fold the top corner down until it meets the napkin's bottom edge, creating a small triangle.

3. Fold the top section about 1/3 of the way down.

4. Fold the napkin in half.

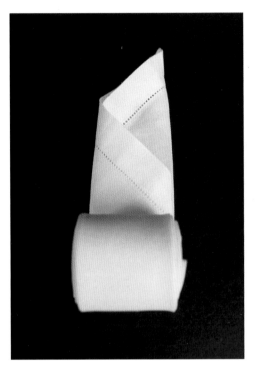

5. Start at one end and carefully roll up the napkin.

6. Wrap ribbon around the rolled napkin to secure the end and place a small flower on top.

A wedding favorite, the Swan can be used at formal holiday dinners or everyday family meals that need a touch of class.

1. Fold the napkin into quarters and place it with the open sides pointing upward.

2. Fold the top corner down until it meets the bottom corner, creating a triangle.

3. Fold the right side of the napkin inward.

4. Repeat with the left side of the napkin, resulting in a kite-like shape.

5. Tuck the top tip of the napkin underneath and turn the napkin so that it is pointing toward the left.

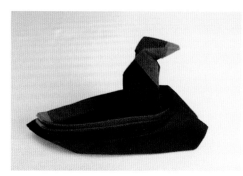

6. Hold the napkin with one hand while you gently pull the swan's neck from the middle of the folded napkin with your other hand. Adjust the tip so it appears pointed to imply the swan's beak.

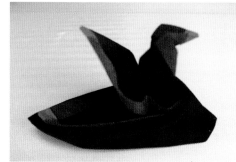

7. Gently pull the next layer created by your fold upward, creating the swan's feathers.

8. Repeat the process, pulling out a second layer.

9. Pull the third layer upward, adjusting as necessary. If desired, decorate the swan with adhesive wiggle eyes.

The Stand

Even the most basic place cards take on a whole new look when they are creatively displayed on The Stand.

1. Fold the napkin in half so that the open end is at the bottom.

2. Fold the top right corner downward, creating a triangle.

3. Repeat the process and fold the top left corner downward, resulting in a large triangle comprised of two smaller triangles.

4. Fold the bottom right corner of the napkin up to the top of the large triangle.

5. Repeat the process on the left side. Fold the bottom left corner of the napkin up to the top of the large triangle.

6. Turn the napkin over.

7. Fold the left and right sides of the napkin inward so they meet in the middle, creating a kite-like shape.

8. Turn the napkin over and carefully pull the back flaps outward on the left and right sides.

9. Fold the right flap downward, tucking it behind the folded napkin.

10. Repeat the process and fold the left flap downward, tucking it behind the folded napkin.

11. Use both hands to stand the napkin and push the flaps to the back.

The Wave

Transform your table with The Wave, which looks wonderful with any color napkin.

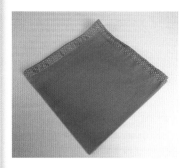

1. Fold the napkin into quarters and place it with the open sides pointing upward.

2. Fold the top layer down to the bottom point of the napkin.

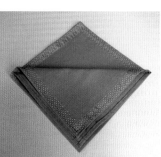

3. Fold the next layer down toward the bottom point of the napkin, leaving a small space between the folded layers.

4. Fold the third layer down toward the bottom point of the napkin, leaving a small space between the folded layers.

5. Fold the final layer downward, creating a triangle, once again leaving a small space between the folded layers.

6. Fold the top right corner of the triangle downward.

7. Repeat the process and fold the top left corner of the triangle downward.

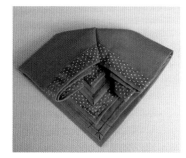

8. Fold the top of the triangle downward behind the napkin to create a flat line along the top.

9. Carefully lift the left and right sides of the napkin upward, using your fingers to separate the layers and create the waves.

Does someone plan on popping the question at dinner? Resembling the inside of a ring box, the Tiffany napkin fold is simple yet elegant.

1. Place the napkin face down in front of you.

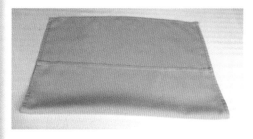

2. Fold 1/3 of the napkin upward.

3. Fold 1/3 of the napkin downward.

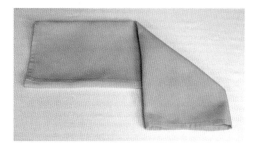

4. Fold the top right corner of the napkin downward until the corner is approximately two inches below the bottom edge.

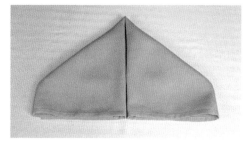

5. Repeat the process and fold the top left corner of the napkin downward until it is approximately two inches below the bottom edge.

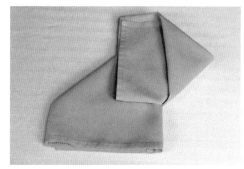

6. Fold the bottom right corner of the napkin upward, creating a triangle with a flap beside it.

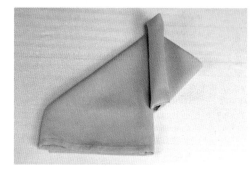

7. Roll the flap toward the right.

8. Fold the bottom left corner of the napkin upward, which will create a corresponding flap on the left side.

9. Roll the flap toward the left, resulting in two columns beside each other. Decorate with jewels or flowers if desired.

Tinker Bell

Appropriate for children's tea parties as well as more adult affairs, Tinker Bell looks ready to fly off the plate!

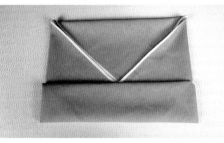

3. Turn the napkin and fold the bottom of the napkin halfway up.

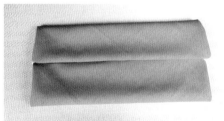

4. Fold the top of the napkin down, meeting the bottom fold.

5. Turn the napkin so that it is vertical and fold approximately 1/4 or 1/3 of the napkin underneath.

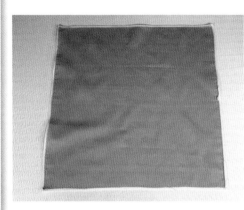

1. Place the napkin face down in front of you.

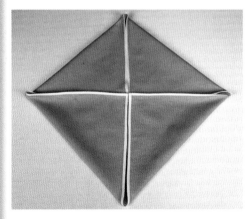

2. Fold the four corners inward so that they meet in the center of the napkin.

6. Fold the left and right sides of the napkin inward.

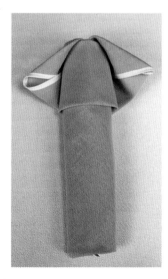

7. Turn the napkin over and carefully adjust Tinker Bell's "wings" as necessary.

Ella

The Tuxedo napkin fold easily corresponds with any color scheme. It is perfect for anniversary parties or other black-tie affairs.

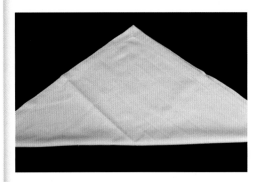

1. Fold the napkin into a triangle by lifting the bottom corner to meet the top corner.

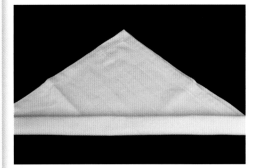

2. Fold the bottom edge of the napkin upward, creating a row that is approximately one-inch thick.

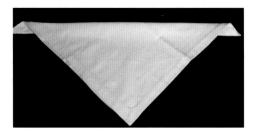

3. Turn the napkin over.

4. Fold the top right corner down until it meets the bottom point of the triangle.

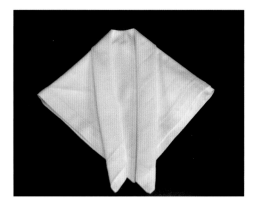

5. Repeat the process and fold the top left corner down until it meets the bottom point of the triangle. Leave a slight gap down the center.

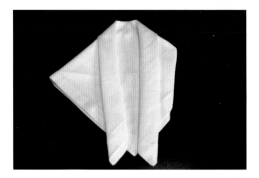

6. Tuck the far right corner underneath the napkin, creating a flat edge along the right side.

7. Repeat the process and tuck the far left corner underneath the napkin, creating a flat edge along the left side.

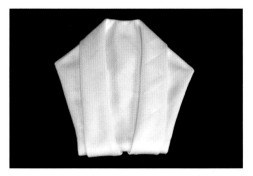

8. Tuck the bottom of the napkin underneath, creating a flat edge along the bottom. Add a bow tie made from ribbon to complete the Tuxedo.

Wedding

The Wedding napkin fold adds timeless grace and elegance to any reception table.

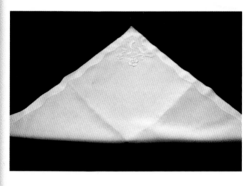

1. Fold the napkin into a triangle by lifting the bottom corner to meet the top corner.

2. Fold the left side of the napkin inward.

3. Repeat with the right side of the napkin.

4. Carefully pull the innermost left layer outward so that it is peeking out.

5. Repeat with the right side of the napkin. Carefully pull the innermost right layer outward so that it is peeking out.

6. Gently lift the center of the napkin upward.

7. Press the lifted center with your hands to create a triangular shape at the bottom of the napkin.

8. Carefully push the sides of the napkin underneath as you pull the center up.

12 Table Setting Designs

Baby Shower

Baby showers have evolved quite a bit over the years and a pastel color palette is no longer an unspoken requirement. Vibrant hues like bright yellow instantly add excitement and energy to the party, especially if baby's arrival is being celebrated in the summertime. Fresh flowers can serve as centerpieces as well as party favors—guests will love bringing home a blossom or two in addition to the usual cookies or candies—and using vivid parrots and geese as table decorations offers a modern escape from the more traditional rubber ducks. If you are not a fan of gender-neutral yellow, consider using fuchsia and hot pink to announce a baby girl or aqua and lime green for a baby boy. A napkin folded into a baby onesie is adorned with ribbon and two small buttons. Matching place cards can be created from card stock or construction paper. The small pacifiers made out of Lifesavers and jelly beans and the baby bottle decorations add a pleasant finishing touch to the table.

Black Tie Affair

Decorations help set the mood for an entire event. Inspired by a loving couple who enjoys ringing in the New Year by dancing the night away, this table setting is ideal for a New Year's Eve celebration or an anniversary soiree. The Tuxedo napkin fold looks appropriately stylish atop black dishes and silver placemats while the checkered tablecloth adds a hint of fun.

White roses alongside black and white candlesticks add an appropriate air of elegance, and the black and white feathers displayed in color-coordinating vases will definitely tickle guests' fancy! The dancing silhouettes, accompanied by cards displaying years, symbolize the past, present, and future.

Chinese Table Setting

A Chinese-themed table setting is an ideal choice for a glamorous Chinese New Year's party or any other dinner featuring Asian food, even if it is take-out from a local restaurant. In Chinese culture, the color red symbolizes good fortune while the color gold represents wealth and happiness. A dark red tablecloth and gold-colored charger plates easily take advantage of these hues. The Orchid in Bloom napkin fold, tucked inside a bowl on each place setting, serves as a functional decoration without distracting from the rest of the table. A conventional Chinese tea set and the use of chopsticks add a bit of authenticity while round candleholders and a golden-hued flower arrangement help achieve a cohesive look. Fortune cookies, though considered an American invention rather than a Chinese tradition, serve as fun conversation pieces and a small bite of dessert.

Wildlife Safari

Holiday dinner parties like those held for Christmas or Thanksgiving can be exciting, but most families have annual traditions they do not like to stray from. Take your guests on a virtual wildlife safari with a zebra-themed dinner celebration, no holiday necessary. A centerpiece of exotic foliage can be as straightforward or complex as you please because any bright colors can complement black and white tables, linens, or room décor such as an animal-print accent rug.

Aside from your flowers or plants, the table decorations can be minimal since the Zebra napkin fold will serve as artwork. Create it from white, black, or patterned napkins and top with your favorite flowers. Who says zoo-themed parties are just for kids?

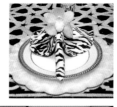

Easter Brunch

Easter tables are fun to create thanks to the abundance of springtime decorations available at most stores. A festive overlay can easily accent plain table linens while Easter eggs—real or artificial—add a welcome splash of color. An Easter egg tree surrounded by ceramic rabbits makes a holiday-appropriate centerpiece. If possible, set the table with plates in a variety of spring colors.

Top with the Bunny in a Hat napkin fold, using stuffed animals or homemade bunnies crafted from card stock. The additions of baby chick and carrot decorations tie in with the overall Easter theme.

Jordan almonds, butter mints, or any other pastel-colored candies instantly turn your candy dishes into art.

Fourth of July

Most Americans take advantage of the opportunity to celebrate freedom on July 4th, our nation's birthday. Casual backyard cookouts are common on Independence Day, but even basic hot dogs and hamburgers somehow taste better when served at a table worthy of its own fireworks display. A tall vase of red, white, and blue flowers surrounded by white metal lanterns and simple pinwheels creates a centerpiece that adds emphasis to the basic blue tablecloth without being overbearing.

White plates adorned with blue stars and the use of blue stemware incorporates the patriotic color scheme while the American Eagle napkin fold puts Old Glory on display in a cheerful manner.

Garden Party

Perfect for Mother's Day, summertime birthday parties, or casual get-togethers, a bright and cheerful garden-themed table is a perfect choice for a buffet-style meal that guests will serve themselves. Yellow carnations and daisies add a touch of nature, giving the impression of an outdoor picnic. Yellow placemats atop a vivid table cloth add brilliance to the room and the Butterfly napkin fold is a favorite among kids of all ages.

Use any color napkins but keep in mind that polka dots are carefree and whimsical. Add pipe cleaner antennae to your butterflies and get ready to see smiles on everyone's faces.

Quinceañera Celebration

Commemorating the transition from childhood to young womanhood when a female turns fifteen, Quinceañera is a tradition celebrated in many Latin American countries and communities. Ceremonies and rituals vary by family and area, but sophisticated balls comparable to wedding receptions are fairly common. Clothing choices may also vary depending on taste and income, but the young woman being honored often wears a pink dress. Regardless of the party's size, a fuchsia color scheme easily adds glamour to the big day. Use solid colored napkins and dark napkin rings to create a Bow napkin fold, perfect for all birthday celebrations, and create centerpieces with dolls wearing pink dresses. Spread color-coordinated candleholders and flowers on the tables and use high heel place cards at each place setting.

Thanksgiving Dinner

Express gratitude among family and friends at a Thanksgiving table that takes advantage of the beauty of autumn. A centerpiece of roses serves as a pleasant diversion from the traditional Thanksgiving cornucopia, but dried corn or other produce still adds ambiance to the table. Pumpkin knickknacks are abundant at this time of year, but a pumpkin-shaped tea set is adorable yet functional. Turkey-shaped salt and pepper shakers are also cute while being practical.

Top the Wave napkin fold with dried leaves and homemade place cards to reinforce the overall Thanksgiving theme.

Valentine's Day Meal

Red roses and Valentine's Day are nearly synonymous, making the England's Rose napkin fold a perfect choice for Valentine's Day brunch or dinner. Rectangular placemats with scalloped edges can replace a traditional tablecloth while still maintaining romantic ambiance. The use of chargers and plates along with stemmed glassware also adds a bit of luxury. Forgo kitschy accessories and keep things simple by adorning the table with functional embellishments like teacups and decorative salt and pepper shakers. A floral arrangement comprised of roses and hydrangeas or your favorite blooms will effortlessly complete the look.

Wedding Reception

Wedding table settings can range from stark to schmaltzy. Achieve a perfect balance between the two with the Wedding napkin fold, which is intricate enough to add tasteful elegance to a modest white tablecloth and basic pastel plates. Matted and framed place cards, along with slip-covered chairs topped with color-coordinating bouquets, also help polish the otherwise simple table. Colored glassware and a bottle of champagne also serve as decoration, as do taper candles and bowls of flowers. Round wedding cakes adorned with ribbon and set atop cake stands add depth and interest—use a table runner for added color and character.

Christmas Dinner Party

Give your traditional Christmas dinner table a makeover with the McEntire's Double Fantasy napkin fold, dedicated to Rev. David McEntire for his kindness and support. Rather than the customary red or green damask tablecloths that are holiday season favorites, use oval-shaped white lace placemats on top of the bare table. They will offer some table protection while acting as decoration. Small statuettes, candlesticks, and short glass vases of red and white flowers decorated with red bows help to balance out the table while maintaining a look of sophisticated simplicity. Larger bows and garland twinkling with white Christmas lights can grace the buffet table or other dining room furniture without looking overbearing.

Decorating with Napkins

Acknowledgments / About the Author

Nothing is more satisfying than showing your working passion in a book. It's literally a dream come true for me. I couldn't have done this myself without the help and support of my multitalented and amazing wife, Lina Ng. I also want to thank my awesome co-writer Melissa Rhone, who has made my life easier. Special thanks to Jean Boles for assisting me with the book; to the Schiffer Publishing staff, especially my editor Jeff Snyder, who is so efficient and helpful. To the design team, you are fantastic! I love my cover. To the good people at Panache, a classic party rental in West Palm Beach, Florida; thank you for letting me do a photo shoot for my table setting diagram. Finally, a very special thank you to the family in Palm Beach who I was privileged to work with for eight years. I cherish every moment, and I am forever grateful.

Touted as the "Napkin Wizard" by the Palm Beach, Florida, press and *Southern Living* magazine, Jimmy Ng has honed his creativity by planning and organizing countless parties—from ultimate family gatherings to wedding receptions for hundreds of people. "The way you decorate your table can make your guests feel welcome and create an atmosphere for a congenial gathering," Jimmy Ng said.

Who knew that napkins could be so special?

Christened "King of the Crease" by the *Palm Beach Post*, Ng is so passionate about napkin folding that he has designed over 300 different ways to enhance a table setting using simple pieces of cloth. He has truly found a "fold" for every occasion.

Ng's fancy creations are a mixture of traditional and original napkin folds. Thanks to twists, tucks, and a whole lot of imagination, he gives napkins and table settings a life of their own.

Ng is no overnight success. He has invested years of hard work in the hospitality arena, a career that has spanned working in catering and managing the homes of Palm Beach families. Ng's desire is to share his talents and techniques: "I want to teach others how to decorate tables in a way that's affordable, easy, yet still chic." He does just that on his website and his popular YouTube channel, where he showcases his talents with step-by-step tutorials.

Jimmy Ng, owner of Napkin Wizard LLC, shares his work with others at NapkinWizard.com. His work has been displayed at The Society of The Four Arts in Palm Beach as well as The Norton Museum of Art in West Palm Beach.

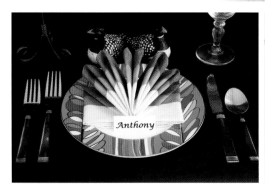